IN TIME OF NEED

A Planning Workbook to Help Families, Friends, and Loved Ones to Prepare for Living and Dying

FRANK KING

Abingdon Press

===== **In Gratitude** =====

To the many who enriched my life by sharing their joys and sorrows in their times of need

Frank G. King

Edited by
Lauren K. Burch
Sheila M. Cole
Roger J. Lapp

Copyright © 1985 by Frank G. King

ICN 189772

All rights reserved.

No part of this work may be reproduced or transmitted in any form or by any means, electronic or mechanical, including photocopying and recording, or by any information storage or retrieval system, except as may be expressly permitted by the 1976 Copyright Act or in writing from the publisher. Requests for permission should be addressed in writing to Abingdon Press, 201 Eighth Avenue South, Nashville, TN 37202.

This book is printed on acid-free paper.

Manufactured by the Parthenon Press at
Nashville, Tennessee, United States of America

ICN 189772

Abingdon Press

Contents

INTRODUCTION

PURPOSE OF THIS BOOK

PART I: COMPILING INFORMATION IN ADVANCE OF THE NEED.......................... 7

    IMPORTANT DOCUMENTS AND THEIR LOCATION.................................. 8

    PERSONAL INFORMATION
        Living Wills.. 12
        Relatives and Friends to Be Notified................................. 15
        Professional/Business People to Be Notified...................... 16
        Funeral and Burial Arrangements..................................... 17
        Obituary Biographical Information.................................... 19
        Provisions for the Care of Dependent Children.................... 20
        Provisions for the Care of Other Dependents..................... 21
        Disposition of Personal Effects.. 22

    BANKING INFORMATION
        Checking Accounts... 23
        Savings Accounts... 24
        Stocks, Bonds, Securities... 25
        Safe Deposit Box Information.. 27
        Trust Funds... 28
        Retirement Accounts... 29
        Certificates of Deposit... 30
        Credit Cards.. 31
        Other Accounts.. 33

    INSURANCE POLICY INFORMATION
        Health Insurance Policies... 35
        Life Insurance Policies... 36
        Business Life Insurance Policies...................................... 37
        Government Life Insurance Policies.................................. 38
        Mortgage Cancellation Insurance Policies......................... 39
        Loan Cancellation Insurance Policies............................... 40

    POSSIBLE BENEFITS INFORMATION
        Employee Death Benefits... 41
        Past Employment Benefits... 42
        Government Benefits.. 43
        Organization Membership Benefits................................... 44

    BUSINESS-RELATED INFORMATION
        Real Estate Owned... 45
        Disposition of Real Estate Property.................................. 46
        Ownership of Businesses, Farms, Franchises..................... 47
        Personal Financial Notes.. 50

PART II: FOR THE FAMILY IN THE TIME OF NEED..51

    NOTIFICATION OF CONCERNED INDIVIDUALS
        Notifying Relatives and Friends..52
        Notifying Employers and Business Associates...52
        Notifying the Funeral Director..52

    FUNERAL AND BURIAL INFORMATION
        Arranging the Funeral Service..53
        Deciding on the Form of Burial...53
        Other Services Provided by the Funeral Director...54
        Prepayment of Funeral and Burial Expenses...54
        Cost of the Funeral and Service..54

    FINANCIAL CONSIDERATION INFORMATION
        Other Expenses and Income That May Be Needed......................................55
        Loss of Income When a Spouse Dies..55
        Funds and Accounts That May Be Frozen Temporarily..................................56
        Possible Sources for Emergency Funds...56
        Possible Sources for Emergency Loans...57
        A Special Note..57

    BENEFITS AND YOUR OPTIONS
        Life Insurance..58
        Accident Insurance...58
        Disability Income Insurance..58
        Employer's Insurance...58
        Social Security Benefits..58
        Veterans Administration Benefits..59
        Insurance Through Organizations...60
        Civil Service Benefits..61

    OTHER CONCERNS
        Debts...62
        Wills...62
        Financial Considerations for the Future..63

PART III: LETTERS TO HELP IN APPLYING FOR SURVIVOR'S BENEFITS................64

    Letter 1-Health Insurance Company..66
    Letter 2-Life Insurance Company...68
    Letter 3-Current Employer..70
    Letter 4-Former Employer..72
    Letter 5-Social Security Office..74
    Letter 6-Veterans Administration..76
    Letter 7-Veterans Administration (Service-Connected Death).......................78
    Letter 8-Organizations..80
    Letter 9-Civil Service Commission...82

Part I
Compiling Information
In Advance of the Need

More times than not, it is necessary for survivors to search for information after a loved one's death. Not only can this be confusing and cause unneeded additional grief, but it can also result in a loss of benefits or estate assets to the survivor(s). This devastating period can be eased if you act *now* to assemble documents and information and record them on the following pages of this workbook.

Information on

_____
Name

_____
Date

Important Documents and Their Location

DOCUMENTS	WHERE LOCATED
Wills	_____
	_____
Insurance Policies	_____
	_____
	_____
	_____
	_____
	_____
Social Security Number	_____
Stocks, Bonds, Securities	_____
	_____
	_____
	_____
	_____
	_____
Marriage Certificate(s)	_____
	_____
	_____
Birth Certificate(s)	_____
	_____

Important Documents and Their Location

DOCUMENTS **WHERE LOCATED**

Military Service Records

Tax Records and Receipts

Car Registration and Title(s)

V.A. Number

Real Estate Deed(s)

Bank Book(s)

Important Documents and Their Location

DOCUMENTS	WHERE LOCATED
Safe Deposit Box(es) and Key(s)	_____
	_____
	_____
Notes Payable and Receivable	_____
	_____
	_____
	_____
Business Contracts and/or Agreements	_____
	_____
	_____
	_____
	_____
	_____
Employment Records	_____
	_____
	_____
	_____
	_____
	_____
	_____
	_____

Important Documents and Their Location

DOCUMENTS

W-2 Forms and Other Records of Earnings

Household Records

Other

WHERE LOCATED

Personal Information

Living Wills

The concern with the conditions in which people approach death is growing. The plight of Karen Ann Quinlan and her family touched many readers. More than the fear of death itself, it is the fear of lingering before death and of creating heavy burdens for families that troubles many. It is also the more general fear of dying in a hospital or nursing home, as more than 80 percent of Americans now must, of a process of growing mental incapacitation perhaps ending in total incompetence, or following prolonged, intense suffering. Underlying all of these fears is that of the loss of the power to affect what happens surrounding the way in which one dies, the power to choose in some measure the place where one wishes to be, and the kind of care one wishes to receive during one's remaining days.

Among the responses to these fears is the effort to state, in advance, how one would like to be treated in the event of terminal illness and inability to make choices for oneself or to see that they are carried out.* Sometimes this decision is made informally in conversations with family members, physicians, and clergy. Such arrangements can be overlooked or give rise to disputes and, therefore, do not always prevail when the time comes to abide by them. Accordingly, a growing number of persons are now signing statements, often known as Living Wills, requesting that their lives not be unduly prolonged under certain conditions.

The legal status of these documents is uncertain. Although they do carry considerable persuasive weight with medical personnel and relatives, they have not yet been recognized as binding by all courts. Several states have legislation pending that would provide such legal recognition. It is likely that they will become increasingly influential as patient autonomy is strengthened and as ways are sought to avoid the dehumanization and suffering that can accompany the ever-growing ability to prolong life to a point that few would wish to reach.

The documents, then, serve several functions. First of all, they represent an effort to retain some control over what happens at the end of one's life, even if one is by then no longer competent to make personal choices or to see that they are carried out. This approach is in recognition of the fact that everyone's choices about when to abandon the struggle for life are not the same. Health professionals might have to assume, in the absence of clear evidence to the contrary, that their patients want the greatest possible effort made to prolong life. In fact, if physicians were to make the contrary assumption without such clear evidence, they might be exposed to civil and criminal liability.

Second, these documents enable individuals to make choices about terminal care while they are still healthy and at a time when there is no doubt of their legal competence.* In this way, health professionals will not have to weight the degree to which the pleas from dying patients represent sustained choices rather than ones influenced by medication, pain, depression, or other deterioration.

*One prerequisite for such choices is that patients have the right to repudiate them at all times.

Third, such statements of requests concerning terminal care can remove, for patients, a burden of choice from a time when many no longer want or have the strength to worry about alternative forms of care. Similarly, much of the anxiety and even guilt on the part of the relatives and health professionals that drives them to provide life support long past the point where the patient might wish for it can be eased by these statements. In the presence of a signed document, no one need feel guilty about stopping short of doing everything possible to delay the moment of death.

This pioneering will has the virtues of brevity and simplicity, but it is vague in such a way that real risk of misinterpretation can arise. A person signing this kind of will has to place great confidence in the kindness of those who will carry it out. Many differ in their interpretation of "physical or mental disability."

This document would make provision, in two ways, for the conflicts that inevitably arise. First of all, it would state that the signer directs that the will should prevail wherever possible unless it is actually unlawful. Second, you may wish to designate a proxy in whom the signer has confidence—a relative, physician, or a trusted friend—to make choices about treatment and to interpret differences if they arise.

The following is a proposal for such a document. Inevitably, some signers will wish to cross out some sentences or add others. Accordingly, deletions should be considered and space for additions provided at the end of the instructions. Statements that some may wish to insert in such a paragraph include requests that medication be provided to alleviate suffering even if the amounts required for relief to be achieved are such as to risk the shortening of life; conditions such as those of paralysis or blindness and degrees of suffering, after which one desires all prolongation of life to cease; circumstances under which one does not wish to enter a hospital or nursing home but rather to be cared for at home; specific instructions concerning where one wishes or does not wish to receive care; procedures that one does not wish to have instituted, perhaps because of moral or religious objections; and the names of physicians, legal counsel, and relatives with whom the document has been discussed.

CONCLUSIONS

There can be no certainty about how one will die. One cannot foretell pace or treatment or ability to cope. This document is not meant to impose more certainty and personal choice on dying than can be had. It is merely an effort to mitigate the worst effects of the uncertainty of those who care for patients without knowing anything about their desires; this uncertainty may force health professionals, in the absence of patient instructions, to do unto others what they would not want anyone to do unto themselves.

Several different forms for Living Wills are available. A widely accepted form follows.

Personal Information

Declaration: Living Will

Declaration made this _____ day of _____ 19____.

I, _____ , willfully and voluntarily make known my desire that my dying shall not be artificially prolonged under the circumstances set forth below and do hereby declare:

If at any time I should have a terminal condition and my attending physician has determined that there can be no recovery from such condition and my death is imminent, where the application of life-prolonging procedures would serve only to artificially prolong the dying process, I direct that such procedure be withheld or withdrawn and that I be permitted to die naturally with only the administration of medication or the performance of any medical procedure deemed necessary to provide me with comfort care or to alleviate pain.

In the absence of my ability to give directions regarding the use of such life-prolonging procedures, it is my intention that this declaration shall be honored by my family and physician as the final expression of my legal right to refuse medical or surgical treatment and accept the consequences for such refusal.

If I have been diagnosed as pregnant and that diagnosis is known to my physician, this declaration shall have no force or effect during the course of my pregnancy.

I understand the full import of this declaration and I am emotionally and mentally competent to make this declaration.

Signed _____

The declarant is known to me and I believe him or her to be of sound mind.

Witness _____

Witness _____

Personal Information

RELATIVES AND FRIENDS TO BE NOTIFIED

Upon the death, the following persons should be notified immediately (names/addresses/phone numbers):

	NAME/ADDRESS	PHONE
1.		
2.		
3.		
4.		
5.		
6.		
7.		
8.		
9.		
10.		
11.		

Personal Information

PROFESSIONAL/BUSINESS PEOPLE TO BE NOTIFIED

Upon the death, the following persons should be notified immediately (names/addresses/phone numbers):

	NAME/ADDRESS	PHONE
Clergy		
Attorney		
Executor		
Business Partners		
Others 1.		
2.		
3.		
4.		
5.		
6.		

Personal Information

FUNERAL AND BURIAL ARRANGEMENTS

Organs to Be Donated _____

_____

Funeral Home Preferred _____

Address of Funeral Home _____

_____ Phone Number _____

Plot Location (owned) or Being Purchased _____

_____

Preferred Cemetery (if plot not already purchased) _____

_____

Burial or Cremation Preference _____

Open or Closed Casket Preference (open for family only, flag draped, etc.). Explain _____

_____

_____

_____

Special Considerations (clothing, jewelry, etc.). Explain _____

_____

Funeral Service Preference

Music _____

_____

_____

Flowers _____

Memorial Gifts (donations to) _____

_____

_____

Personal Information

FUNERAL AND BURIAL ARRANGEMENTS

Pallbearers

NAME/ADDRESS **PHONE**

1. _____ _____
   _____

2. _____ _____
   _____

3. _____ _____
   _____

4. _____ _____
   _____

5. _____ _____
   _____

6. _____ _____
   _____

Person(s) to Give Eulogies

1. _____ _____
   _____

2. _____ _____
   _____

3. _____ _____
   _____

Other Preferences

_____

_____

Personal Information

OBITUARY BIOGRAPHICAL INFORMATION

Date of Birth _____ Place of Birth _____

Date of Death _____ Place of Death _____

Business/Employed by _____

Personal Achievements _____

_____

_____

_____

_____

_____

_____

_____

Memberships Held _____

_____

_____

_____

_____

_____

Immediate Family _____

_____

_____

Parents _____

Personal Information

PROVISIONS FOR THE CARE OF DEPENDENT CHILDREN

In the event that my spouse and I die while our children are minors, the following arrangements have been made in their behalf (names, relationships, addresses, telephone numbers of guardian[s]):

_____
_____
_____
_____
_____
_____
_____

No arrangements have been made to date, but my spouse and I hope that the following arrangements can be made:

_____
_____
_____
_____
_____
_____
_____

Trust(s) That Have Been Set Up
_____
_____
_____

The Bank or Trust Company Is
_____
_____

Personal Information

PROVISIONS FOR THE CARE OF OTHER DEPENDENTS

Name _____

Relationship _____

_____

Address _____

_____

Arrangements Made _____

_____

_____

_____

_____

_____

_____

_____

_____

_____

_____

Trust(s) That Have Been Set Up

_____

_____

_____

The Bank or Trust Company Is

_____

_____

Personal Information

DISPOSITION OF PERSONAL EFFECTS OF _____

Distribution As Follows:

Items	Who to Receive Them
_____	_____
_____	_____
_____	_____
_____	_____
_____	_____
_____	_____
_____	_____
_____	_____
_____	_____
_____	_____
_____	_____
_____	_____
_____	_____

Remember: Church, Congregation, Mission Programs: _____

_____

_____

Also Remember: Charities, Schools, Organ Donations (see "Wills" on page 62): _____

_____

Banking Information

CHECKING ACCOUNT(S)

Name(s) Held In _____

Account Number _____

Name and Location of Bank/S&L _____

_____

Location of Documents (checkbook, statements, etc.) _____

_____

CHECKING ACCOUNT(S)

Name(s) Held In _____

Account Number _____

Name and Location of Bank/S&L _____

_____

Location of Documents (checkbook, statements, etc.) _____

_____

CHECKING ACCOUNT(S)

Name(s) Held In _____

Account Number _____

Name and Location of Bank/S&L _____

_____

Location of Documents (checkbook, statements, etc.) _____

_____

Note: States have different laws and statutes dealing with various ownership.

Banking Information

SAVINGS ACCOUNT(S)

Name(s) Held In _____

Account Number _____

Name and Location of Bank/S&L _____

_____

Location of Documents (passbook, statements, etc.) _____

_____

SAVINGS ACCOUNT(S)

Name(s) Held In _____

Account Number _____

Name and Location of Bank/S&L _____

_____

Location of Documents (passbook, statements, etc.) _____

_____

SAVINGS ACCOUNT(S)

Name(s) Held In _____

Account Number _____

Name and Location of Bank/S&L _____

_____

Location of Documents (passbook, statements, etc.) _____

_____

Note: States have different laws and statutes dealing with various ownership.

Banking Information

STOCKS, BONDS, SECURITIES

Name(s) Held In _____

Name(s) of Company on Certificate _____

Name and Location of Broker and Brokerage _____

_____

Location of Documents _____

_____

STOCKS, BONDS, SECURITIES

Name(s) Held In _____

Name(s) of Company on Certificate _____

Name and Location of Broker and Brokerage _____

_____

Location of Documents _____

_____

STOCKS, BONDS, SECURITIES

Name(s) Held In _____

Name(s) of Company on Certificate _____

Name and Location of Broker and Brokerage _____

_____

Location of Documents _____

_____

Note: States have different laws and statutes dealing with various ownership.

Banking Information

STOCKS, BONDS, SECURITIES

Name(s) Held In _____

Name(s) of Company on Certificate _____

Name and Location of Broker and Brokerage _____

_____

Location of Documents _____

_____

STOCKS, BONDS, SECURITIES

Name(s) Held In _____

Name(s) of Company on Certificate _____

Name and Location of Broker and Brokerage _____

_____

Location of Documents _____

_____

STOCKS, BONDS, SECURITIES

Name(s) Held In _____

Name(s) of Company on Certificate _____

Name and Location of Broker and Brokerage _____

_____

Location of Documents _____

_____

Note: States have different laws and statutes dealing with various ownership.

Banking Information

SAFE DEPOSIT BOX INFORMATION

Name(s) Held In _____

Account Number _____

Box Number _____

Name and Location of Bank/S&L _____

_____

Location of Documents (keys, book, statements, etc.) _____

_____

SAFE DEPOSIT BOX INFORMATION

Name(s) Held In _____

Account Number _____

Box Number _____

Name and Location of Bank/S&L _____

_____

Location of Documents (keys, book, statements, etc.) _____

_____

SAFE DEPOSIT BOX INFORMATION

Name(s) Held In _____

Account Number _____

Box Number _____

Name and Location of Bank/S&L _____

_____

Location of Documents (keys, book, statements, etc.) _____

_____

Note: States have different laws and statutes dealing with various ownership.

Banking Information

TRUST FUND(S)

Name(s) Held In _____

Account Number _____

Name and Location of Bank/S&L _____

_____

Location of Documents (statements, etc.) _____

_____

TRUST FUND(S)

Name(s) Held In _____

Account Number _____

Name and Location of Bank/S&L _____

_____

Location of Documents (statements, etc.) _____

_____

TRUST FUND(S)

Name(s) Held In _____

Account Number _____

Name and Location of Bank/S&L _____

_____

Location of Documents (statements, etc.) _____

_____

Note: States have different laws and statutes dealing with various ownership.

Banking Information

RETIREMENT ACCOUNT(S)

Name(s) Held In _____

Account Number _____

Name and Location of Bank/S&L _____

_____

Location of Documents (statements, etc.) _____

_____

RETIREMENT ACCOUNT(S)

Name(s) Held In _____

Account Number _____

Name and Location of Bank/S&L _____

_____

Location of Documents (statements, etc.) _____

_____

RETIREMENT ACCOUNT(S)

Name(s) Held In _____

Account Number _____

Name and Location of Bank/S&L _____

_____

Location of Documents (statements, etc.) _____

_____

Note: States have different laws and statutes dealing with various ownership.

Banking Information

CERTIFICATES OF DEPOSIT

Name(s) Held In _____

Account Number _____

Name and Location of Bank/S&L _____

_____

Location of Documents (checkbook, statements, etc.) _____

_____

CERTIFICATES OF DEPOSIT

Name(s) Held In _____

Account Number _____

Name and Location of Bank/S&L _____

_____

Location of Documents (checkbook, statements, etc.) _____

_____

CERTIFICATES OF DEPOSIT

Name(s) Held In _____

Account Number _____

Name and Location of Bank/S&L _____

_____

Location of Documents (checkbook, statements, etc.) _____

_____

Note: States have different laws and statutes dealing with various ownership.

Banking Information

CREDIT CARD(S)

Name(s) Held In _____

Account Number _____

Name and Location of Bank/Institution _____

_____

Location of Documents (agreements, statements, etc.) _____

_____

CREDIT CARD(S)

Name(s) Held In _____

Account Number _____

Name and Location of Bank/Institution _____

_____

Location of Documents (agreements, statements, etc.) _____

_____

CREDIT CARD(S)

Name(s) Held In _____

Account Number _____

Name and Location of Bank/Institution _____

_____

Location of Documents (agreements, statements, etc.) _____

_____

Note: States have different laws and statutes dealing with various ownership.

Banking Information

CREDIT CARD(S)

Name(s) Held In _____

Account Number _____

Name and Location of Bank/Institution _____

_____

Location of Documents (agreements, statements, etc.) _____

_____

CREDIT CARD(S)

Name(s) Held In _____

Account Number _____

Name and Location of Bank/Institution _____

_____

Location of Documents (agreements, statements, etc.) _____

_____

CREDIT CARD(S)

Name(s) Held In _____

Account Number _____

Name and Location of Bank/Institution _____

_____

Location of Documents (agreements, statements, etc.) _____

_____

Note: States have different laws and statutes dealing with various ownership.

Banking Information

OTHER ACCOUNT(S)

Name(s) Held In _____

Account Number _____

Name and Location of Bank/S&L _____

_____

Location of Documents (statements, etc.) _____

_____

OTHER ACCOUNT(S)

Name(s) Held In _____

Account Number _____

Name and Location of Bank/S&L _____

_____

Location of Documents (statements, etc.) _____

_____

OTHER ACCOUNT(S)

Name(s) Held In _____

Account Number _____

Name and Location of Bank/S&L _____

_____

Location of Documents (statements, etc.) _____

_____

Note: States have different laws and statutes dealing with various ownership.

Banking Information

OTHER ACCOUNT(S)

Name(s) Held In _____

Account Number _____

Name and Location of Bank/S&L _____

_____

Location of Documents (statements, etc.) _____

_____

OTHER ACCOUNT(S)

Name(s) Held In _____

Account Number _____

Name and Location of Bank/S&L _____

_____

Location of Documents (statements, etc.) _____

_____

OTHER ACCOUNT(S)

Name(s) Held In _____

Account Number _____

Name and Location of Bank/S&L _____

_____

Location of Documents (statements, etc.) _____

_____

Note: States have different laws and statutes dealing with various ownership.

Insurance Policy Information

HEALTH INSURANCE POLICIES

Person Insured _____

Beneficiary _____

Insurance Company _____ Policy Number _____

Policy Location _____

Type (group, major medical, supplemental, etc.) _____

Person Insured _____

Beneficiary _____

Insurance Company _____ Policy Number _____

Policy Location _____

Type (group, major medical, supplemental, etc.) _____

Person Insured _____

Beneficiary _____

Insurance Company _____ Policy Number _____

Policy Location _____

Type (group, major medical, supplemental, etc.) _____

Person Insured _____

Beneficiary _____

Insurance Company _____ Policy Number _____

Policy Location _____

Type (group, major medical, supplemental, etc.) _____

Insurance Policy Information

LIFE INSURANCE POLICIES

Person Insured _____

Beneficiary _____

Insurance Company _____ Policy Number _____

Policy Location _____

Face Value _____

Person Insured _____

Beneficiary _____

Insurance Company _____ Policy Number _____

Policy Location _____

Face Value _____

Person Insured _____

Beneficiary _____

Insurance Company _____ Policy Number _____

Policy Location _____

Face Value _____

Person Insured _____

Beneficiary _____

Insurance Company _____ Policy Number _____

Policy Location _____

Face Value _____

Insurance Policy Information

BUSINESS LIFE INSURANCE POLICIES

Person Insured _____

Beneficiary _____

Insurance Company _____ Policy Number _____

Policy Location _____

Face Value _____

Person Insured _____

Beneficiary _____

Insurance Company _____ Policy Number _____

Policy Location _____

Face Value _____

Person Insured _____

Beneficiary _____

Insurance Company _____ Policy Number _____

Policy Location _____

Face Value _____

Person Insured _____

Beneficiary _____

Insurance Company _____ Policy Number _____

Policy Location _____

Face Value _____

Insurance Policy Information

GOVERNMENT LIFE INSURANCE POLICIES

Branch of Service _____

Served From _____ To _____

Type of Discharge _____

Serial Number _____

Status of Government Life Insurance: Expired _____ In Force _____

Face Value _____

Beneficiary _____

Policy Location _____

VFW/American Legion Benefits _____

Location of Discharge Papers _____

Insurance Policy Information

MORTGAGE CANCELLATION INSURANCE POLICIES

Person Insured _____

Beneficiary _____

Insurance Company _____ Policy Number _____

Policy Location _____

Item Insured _____

Person Insured _____

Beneficiary _____

Insurance Company _____ Policy Number _____

Policy Location _____

Item Insured _____

Person Insured _____

Beneficiary _____

Insurance Company _____ Policy Number _____

Policy Location _____

Item Insured _____

Person Insured _____

Beneficiary _____

Insurance Company _____ Policy Number _____

Policy Location _____

Item Insured _____

Insurance Policy Information

LOAN CANCELLATION INSURANCE POLICIES

Person Insured _____

Beneficiary _____

Insurance Company _____ Policy Number _____

Policy Location _____

Property Location _____

Person Insured _____

Beneficiary _____

Insurance Company _____ Policy Number _____

Policy Location _____

Property Location _____

Person Insured _____

Beneficiary _____

Insurance Company _____ Policy Number _____

Policy Location _____

Property Location _____

Person Insured _____

Beneficiary _____

Insurance Company _____ Policy Number _____

Policy Location _____

Property Location _____

For example, credit life, auto, boat, appliance.

Possible Benefits Information

EMPLOYEE DEATH BENEFITS

Present Employer _____

Address _____

Phone Numbers _____

Survivors are eligible for the following benefits from my employer/company upon death:

☐ Pension Benefits	☐ Unpaid Accrued Vacation
☐ Group Life Insurance	☐ Unused Accrued Sick Leave
☐ Profit-Sharing Plans	☐ Unpaid Salary
☐ Credit Union Holdings	☐ Travel Insurance
☐ Deferred Compensation Arrangements	☐ Worker's Compensation

☐ Disability _____

☐ Other _____

Present Employer _____

Address _____

Phone Numbers _____

Survivors are eligible for the following benefits from my employer/company upon death:

☐ Pension Benefits	☐ Unpaid Accrued Vacation
☐ Group Life Insurance	☐ Unused Accrued Sick Leave
☐ Profit-Sharing Plans	☐ Unpaid Salary
☐ Credit Union Holdings	☐ Travel Insurance
☐ Deferred Compensation Arrangements	☐ Worker's Compensation

☐ Disability _____

☐ Other _____

Possible Benefits Information

PAST EMPLOYMENT BENEFITS

Employer _____

Address _____

Dates Employed _____

Possible Benefits _____

_____

Employer _____

Address _____

Dates Employed _____

Possible Benefits _____

_____

Employer _____

Address _____

Dates Employed _____

Possible Benefits _____

_____

Employer _____

Address _____

Dates Employed _____

Possible Benefits _____

_____

Possible Benefits Information

GOVERNMENT BENEFITS

Family is eligible for benefits through:

☐ Railroad Retirement _____

Dates _____

Document Location _____

☐ Active Military or Veteran's Service-connected Death _____

Dates _____

Document Location _____

☐ Civil Service _____

Dates _____

Document Location _____

☐ Veteran's Nonservice-connected Death _____

Dates _____

Document Location _____

☐ Benefits from State or Local Government _____

Dates _____

Document Location _____

☐ Social Security Benefits _____

Dates _____

Document Location _____

Possible Benefits Information

ORGANIZATION MEMBERSHIP BENEFITS

Due to memberships in certain organizations (fraternal, unions, church, etc.), survivors may be eligible for some benefits.

Organization _____

Address _____

Type of Benefits _____

Location of Membership Records _____

Organization _____

Address _____

Type of Benefits _____

Location of Membership Records _____

Organization _____

Address _____

Type of Benefits _____

Location of Membership Records _____

Organization _____

Address _____

Type of Benefits _____

Location of Membership Records _____

Organization _____

Address _____

Type of Benefits _____

Location of Membership Records _____

Business-related Information

REAL ESTATE OWNED

Primary Residence _____
_____

Owned: Jointly with spouse _____

    Jointly with nonspouse _____

    Singly by _____

Mortgagor _____

Location of Records _____

Other Real Estate: Type _____

Address _____

Owned: Jointly with spouse _____

    Jointly with nonspouse _____

    Singly by _____

Mortgagor _____

Location of Records _____

Other Real Estate: Type _____

Address _____

Owned: Jointly with spouse _____

    Jointly with nonspouse _____

    Singly by _____

Mortgagor _____

Location of Records _____

Business-related Information

DISPOSITION OF REAL ESTATE PROPERTY OF _____

Location   Who to Receive It

Business-related Information

OWNERSHIP OF BUSINESSES, FARMS, FRANCHISES

Name of Business _____

Kind of Business _____

Location _____

Percentage of Ownership (%) _____

Form of Business (sole proprietorship/partnership, closed corporate) _____
_____

Other Owners (if any) _____
_____
_____
_____
_____

Arrangements that have been made or should be made in continuing or disposing of each business interest _____
_____
_____
_____
_____
_____

Location of papers/books/records, etc., pertaining to business _____
_____
_____

Person(s) who could offer sound advice concerning the business/farm _____
_____
_____

Additional Pertinent Information _____
_____

Business-related Information

OWNERSHIP OF BUSINESSES, FARMS, FRANCHISES

Name of Business _____

Kind of Business _____

Location _____

Percentage of Ownership (%) _____

Form of Business (sole proprietorship/partnership, closed corporate) _____

_____

Other Owners (if any) _____

_____

_____

_____

Arrangements that have been made or should be made in continuing or disposing of each business interest _____

_____

_____

_____

_____

Location of papers/books/records, etc., pertaining to business _____

_____

_____

Person(s) who could offer sound advice concerning the business/farm _____

_____

_____

Additional Pertinent Information _____

_____

Business-related Information

OWNERSHIP OF BUSINESSES, FARMS, FRANCHISES

Name of Business _____

Kind of Business _____

Location _____

Percentage of Ownership (%) _____

Form of Business (sole proprietorship/partnership, closed corporate) _____

Other Owners (if any) _____

_____

_____

_____

Arrangements that have been made or should be made in continuing or disposing of each business interest _____

_____

_____

_____

_____

Location of papers/books/records, etc., pertaining to business _____

_____

Person(s) who could offer sound advice concerning the business/farm _____

_____

_____

Additional Pertinent Information _____

_____

Business-related Information

PERSONAL FINANCIAL NOTES

Money Owed to Me by _____

Location of Documentation _____

Money Owed to Me by _____

Location of Documentation _____

Money Owed to Me by _____

Location of Documentation _____

Money Owed to Me by _____

Location of Documentation _____

Money I Owe (to whom) _____

Location of Documentation _____

Money I Owe (to whom) _____

Location of Documentation _____

Money I Owe (to whom) _____

Location of Documentation _____

Money I Owe (to whom) _____

Location of Documentation _____

Location of Equity Held (i.e., pawned items) _____

_____

_____

Part II
For the Family in the Time of Need

The death of a loved one has occurred. Part II is designed as a guideline to help the deceased's family move less stressfully through the difficult days and weeks that immediately follow the death. Now is the time to use the information compiled in part I.

Notification of Concerned Individuals

NOTIFYING RELATIVES AND FRIENDS

Having to notify relatives and friends of a loved one's death is never easy. When it comes to someone you were also very close to, it is even harder, and because you are the closest, you will be very vulnerable. Allow your friends to help and support you in their own way. At this time you won't want to think about everyday things in your life. This is where friends can be especially helpful. Remember, they probably are hurting too, and in helping you, they feel needed, which in turn helps them.

When you, your immediate family, and helper friends start to notify people, those people will have questions. Be prepared for this. Make a list beforehand of the information they may want to know (funeral arrangements, etc.), and let them know where you can be reached.

The first people who should be notified are those the deceased was particularly close to, usually the family. Be aware of those people who must be called who suffer from ill health and for whom the news could prove particularly devastating. In these cases, it is better that someone tell them in person rather than they hear the news on the phone when they may be alone.

In part I, page 15, a list should have been compiled of those people to be notified. Refer to this. This is the time for which the list was compiled.

Next to be notified, after the close family, are particularly close friends, then other family members and friends. It is not always easy to know who takes priority at this time, but those who were closest should be notified first.

NOTIFYING EMPLOYERS AND BUSINESS ASSOCIATES

Employers and business associates will want to know as soon as possible in order to pay their respects to the family. Some may be close friends who can help notify other friends about the death. Quick notification also gives the deceased's employer a chance to begin reviewing the records to see what company benefits are available to you and your family.

NOTIFYING THE FUNERAL DIRECTOR

If no arrangements have been previously made, contact a funeral home close to your home address regardless of where the death takes place. The funeral home will help with arrangements. If the death is out of town, the hometown funeral home will take charge of having the body returned to your city.

Funeral and Burial Information

ARRANGING THE FUNERAL SERVICE

It is to be hoped that because of this workbook, you and your spouse/dependent(s) have discussed funeral arrangements ahead of time so that you will know exactly what kind of service to have. If not, the funeral directors will explain the various alternatives available and let you select arrangements that you feel would be in keeping with the deceased's wishes.

The funeral director will take responsibility for completing the death certificate, obtaining the burial permit, and sending a death notice to the local newspapers. He/she will also contact others who should be involved in the service, such as your clergyman, pallbearers, etc. By handling all necessary arrangements, he/she can free you of much of the burden of the funeral and leave you time to be with friends and relatives during this most difficult period.

If you prefer, your clergyman can be called upon to help make the decisions. Among the things that you will need to decide with the funeral director are

- What kind of casket to have
- When to have visitation hours
- What type of service to have (religious, fraternal, memorial, etc.)
- What ethnic customs should be observed
- Where the service is to be held (church, funeral home, or elsewhere)
- Who is to conduct the service (clergyman, fellow lodge member, friend, military service)
- What to include in the service (eulogy, Scripture, music, etc.)
- Whom to have as pallbearers and perhaps honorary pallbearers

DECIDING ON THE FORM OF BURIAL

Unless arrangements have been made ahead of time, the funeral director can help you decide on the final resting place for the deceased and can help make the necessary arrangements in accordance with your or the deceased's wishes. Following are the choices to be considered:

- Earth burial: You will need to choose a cemetery, purchase a cemetery lot, select a burial receptacle, and decide on what (if any) kind of marker or monument to have. (A decision on the marker can be made immediately or later.)
- Entombment: You will need to select a mausoleum and purchase a crypt.
- Cremation: You will need to decide what disposition is to be made of the cremated remains. This may also mean purchasing an urn and buying a niche in a columbarium to hold the urn.

If the final disposition of the body or ashes is to be in another city or state, the funeral director can handle transportation of the casket or urn to the site, make travel arrangements for the family, and coordinate details with an affiliated funeral home, which will handle arrangements locally (such as purchasing a cemetery lot, conducting graveside services, etc.).

Funeral and Burial Information

OTHER SERVICES PROVIDED BY THE FUNERAL DIRECTOR

There are numerous other services the local funeral director performs:

- He notifies the coroner, when necessary, for accidental or violent death or if death takes place at home.
- He completes the death certificate and has the attending physician certify the medical cause of death.
- He obtains a burial permit from the local registrar.
- If an autopsy is required by law or requested by the family physician, he will make the necessary arrangements with your written consent.
- If organs are to be donated, he cooperates with the hospitals, physicians, and organizations.
- He sends a death notice to the local newspapers and provides them with more extensive information for an obituary.
- Upon request, he will help with processing certain claims and completing various other forms.

If you have need of any of these services, let the director know.

PREPAYMENT OF FUNERAL AND BURIAL EXPENSES

While some people take out burial insurance policies to cover these expenses, others join burial societies for the same purpose. In another type of arrangement where the funeral services are preplanned, one has the option of paying the expenses in advance. In this case, the money for the service is placed in a trust fund until needed. Whichever method of prepayment is chosen, the document specifying this should be kept with other policies and survivor(s) should be notified in advance of its existence (see part I).

COST OF THE FUNERAL AND SERVICE

The price of a funeral, including burial, usually includes the casket, professional services of the funeral home, rental of the funeral home's facilities, use of a hearse, and so forth, and is referred to as "total adult service." Most funeral homes have several different services available, and you select the one in the price range best suited to your wishes and ability to pay. Costs differ in various parts of the country. Miscellaneous expenses not included in the price of the funeral consist of such items as an honorarium for the person conducting the service, flowers, and paid newspaper death notices.

It might be a good idea to seek the advice of an attorney in deciding which method of payment to choose for the funeral, burial, and related costs.

Financial Consideration Information

OTHER EXPENSES AND INCOME THAT MAY BE NEEDED

More money than usual may be needed during the week of the funeral.

Possible expenses during the week of the funeral include long-distance telephone calls to friends and relatives, food and drink for visitors to your home, and mourning clothing needed for the immediate family for the funeral.

During the weeks after the funeral, you may have certain other expenses, such as fees connected with filing claims, extra travel expenses, long-distance telephone calls, increased expenses for meals, and a babysitter for young children while you are making trips around town to get various matters resolved.

Furthermore, during this period most of the current living costs and obligations of the family will continue, including food, mortgage or rent payments, utilities (heating oil, electricity, gas, and telephone), automobile operation expenses, insurance premiums on home and automobile, life insurance premiums on the family, clothing, laundry and dry cleaning, drugs and prescriptions, minor miscellaneous expenses (children's allowances, expenses at school, newspapers, magazines, etc.).

Note: You may wish to show your attorney all bills and notices that come in. He or she will advise you which should be paid and which represent claims against the estate and should therefore be dealt with later as part of the probate process.

LOSS OF INCOME WHEN A SPOUSE DIES

As can be seen, the death of a loved one causes additional expenses over and above the normal living expenses for the family.

When the deceased is a spouse who had an outside income, additional problems may occur. The income ceases. Expenses, therefore, cannot be paid from it. Even if the surviving spouse has an income, he or she may not want to work during this very emotional time, and the income can possibly cease here also.

Although benefits such as Social Security may be due, it will take time for them to begin providing a regular monthly income.

What this means, then, is that a considerable amount of cash is going to be needed during the first couple of months following a spouse's death and that the money will have to be raised very quickly. However, the following sources of money that may have been readily available to the family while the spouse was alive may now be inaccessible for a while.

Financial Consideration Information

FUNDS AND ACCOUNTS THAT MAY BE TEMPORARILY FROZEN

- Joint checking account: In most states the law requires the bank to stop payment of any checks drawn on a joint bank account once the bank learns of either party's death. Talk with the banker immediately. The bank will notify the tax authorities so that a sizable amount of the account can be released as soon as possible to help pay for living expenses.
- Joint savings account: This money, too, may be frozen. File a request for release of funds with the bank so that all or some of this money is available if needed during the immediate postdeath period.
- Safe deposit box: It may be sealed upon a spouse's death and will remain sealed until the contents are inventoried by the tax appraiser. Inventorying may be done immediately or at the mutual convenience of the concerned parties. Thereafter, the court-appointed executor may use such funds for estate purposes, including partial distribution to the widow/widower.

In addition to the above, many of the other assets that a spouse may own or that have been jointly owned may be frozen until probate. There are several reasons the law requires this conservation of the assets until the estate is probated. These include (1) determining what federal and state taxes must be paid, (2) protecting the just claims of creditors, and (3) protecting the interests of the heirs.

Be wary of raising immediate cash by selling anything owned by the deceased(s). An attorney or the clerk or the probate court can inform you in general terms of which assets will be included in the probate process and which will not. Once it is known which property will pass directly to the survivor(s), it can be determined what assets can be used to help meet immediate expenses.

POSSIBLE SOURCES FOR EMERGENCY FUNDS

Normally the following, if available, can be used for daily living expenses and other costs incurred during the first two months or so following a spouse's death.

- Checking or savings accounts in the survivor's name
- Credit cards
- U.S. Savings Bonds
- The deceased's employer
- Life insurance
- Trusts

Financial Consideration Information

POSSIBLE SOURCES FOR EMERGENCY LOANS

If you cannot raise the money you need from the sources discussed previously, the following may be able to assist you with an emergency loan.

- Relatives
- Bank
- Red Cross
- Salvation Army
- Social services organizations and welfare agencies
- Church/Synagogue

A SPECIAL NOTE

In the effort to raise cash for current living expenses and the additional expenses incurred during the period immediately following a death, be very careful not to waste money. Recognize the fact that possibly a main source of income has been cut off because of the death and a regular income will be needed for many years into the future. Do not make any ill-considered or unnecessary expenditures of precious cash during this immediate postdeath period. Spend sparingly until you have had a chance to begin recovering your emotional balance and have time to make a thorough study of your changed financial picture.

Benefits and Your Options

LIFE INSURANCE

Life and health insurance companies sell a variety of individual coverages, including life insurance, annuities, accident insurance, and disability income insurance. Have your life insurance agent go through all of the deceased's policies with you to see what coverages are provided, how much money is available from each policy, and how those proceeds are to be disbursed.

Make sure you have a very clear picture of the settlement options available under each policy and that you understand what your needs will be before you decide on an option. This is very important. Remember, once you elect to take the proceeds of a policy under certain options or take the money in a lump sum, you cannot change your mind and elect another option.

If you are undecided, a good alternative is to use the "interest option," which permits you to collect the interest on the proceeds the company is holding for you. Later, when you have decided, you can exercise your right to have the proceeds paid out to you under one of the options previously mentioned.

Note: You may want to have an attorney involved in the decision about selecting settlement options. Some of this insurance money may be needed to pay federal estate taxes, state inheritance taxes, the current year's income taxes, and so forth.

ACCIDENT INSURANCE

In the event the deceased died an accidental death and owned an accident insurance policy, there may be a death benefit payable to the named beneficiary. Check with your agent, as some policies pay only under certain conditions.

DISABILITY INCOME INSURANCE

Some of these policies pay a death benefit in the event the insured dies an accidental death. If the deceased had disability income insurance, ask your agent if the policy has this feature.

EMPLOYER'S INSURANCE

Many employers carry an insurance policy on their employees usually equal to one year's pay.

SOCIAL SECURITY BENEFITS

In many homes where there is either an elderly survivor or a survivor with young children, monthly Social Security checks may be a major source of income. If your spouse was covered under Social Security, check with the local office of the Social Security Administration to see who, if anyone, in your family is entitled to benefits at the present time and approximately how much those benefits will be.

Typically, the eligible survivors of a worker who was covered under Social Security include dependent children under age eighteen (or age twenty-two if a full-time college student) and the widow or widower over the age of sixty.

The major factors in determining the amount of benefits include your spouse's income, the length of time Social Security taxes were paid, and the number of dependent children. If there are no dependent children, a survivor can apply for a full benefit at age sixty-five.

Remember, those monthly checks from Social Security do not start coming in automatically to eligible survivors following the "covered worker's" death. **They must be applied for. If you and/or your children are eligible for Social Security benefits, do not delay in filing for them. It will take between one and three months from the date you apply until the first check arrives.**

DOCUMENTS AND FORMS NEEDED TO FILE FOR SOCIAL SECURITY BENEFITS

- A certified copy of the death certificate
- The deceased's Social Security number
- The Social Security numbers of yourself and your dependent children
- Your wedding certificate
- Birth certificates for yourself and your dependent children
- Your spouse's tax records for the past year or some other record of the previous year's earnings

VETERANS ADMINISTRATION BENEFITS

If the deceased was a veteran of the armed forces, he or she probably had government life insurance while in the service, and this insurance may still be in force.

There have been a number of government life insurance programs in effect at various times since World War I. Describing the kinds of policies issued over the years would be beyond the scope of this publication. However, on all of the policies, various settlement options are available, in addition to lump-sum payment, usually electable only by the insured. If the deceased had any type of government life insurance policy in force at the time of death, either your own life insurance agent or the local office of the Veterans Administration can explain the provisions of the policy to you and help you decide which settlement option to elect.

In addition to life insurance, a spouse and dependent may be eligible for certain other benefits from the Veterans Administration. For example, if the deceased veteran (not dishonorably discharged) had a service-connected disability, the spouse and dependent children may be eligible to receive educational assistance under the War Orphans' and Widows' Educational Assistance Act. Also, his/her survivor may be able to qualify for a GI home loan and, until remarried, get a ten-point preference in hiring when applying for a civil service position.

Benefits and Your Options

Finally, whether or not the deceased veteran had a service-connected disability, the spouse or dependent children may be eligible for a pension from the Veterans Administration. However, anyone applying for such payments must have a very low income in order to qualify for the pension.

FILING FOR VETERANS BENEFITS

Write to the Insurance Division of the Veterans Administration Center nearest to you for an insurance claim form. (Use letter 6 in part III). You can also write the Veterans Administration Center to inquire about any other benefit to which you may be entitled (using letter 7). There are two such centers, one in Philadelphia and the other in St. Paul. Their addresses are 500 Wissachickon Avenue, Philadelphia, PA 19019, and Fort Snelling, St. Paul, MN 55111. An alternative procedure would be to contact your local Veterans Administration Office for information about benefits and assistance in applying for them.

DOCUMENTS NEEDED TO FILE FOR VETERANS ADMINISTRATION BENEFITS

- A copy of the deceased's discharge from the service
- A copy of the death certificate, unless death occurred in a Veterans Administration hospital
- A copy of your marriage certificate
- Copies of your dependent children's birth certificates
- The deceased's Veterans Administration claim number

Note: If the deceased was on active duty in the armed forces at the time of death, or if death was service connected, a number of government benefits may be available. Three kinds of death benefits are burial allowance, lump-sum death gratuity, and compensation for spouse, children, and dependent parents.

The Veterans Administration and the various branches of the service share in the administration of benefits for the families of deceased veterans. For detailed information, consult your nearest Veterans Administration office and write to the headquarters office of the deceased's branch of service in Washington, D.C.

INSURANCE THROUGH ORGANIZATIONS

Was the deceased a member of a union, professional society, vocational or trade association, fraternal benefit society, business association, automobile club, or any other type of organization? If so, be sure to check with that group to see what benefits they offer members and which, if any, of these benefits will be made available to the spouse and children. Possibilities include life insurance, health coverages with a "principal sum" (accidental death benefit), pension plan (with either pension payments or a lump sum benefit for the widow/widower), special death benefit for member's family, credit union, and return of unused annual dues.

If the deceased was a member of such an organization, you will also want to locate any policies, certificates, and other valuable papers pertaining to membership benefits (use letter 8).

DOCUMENTS AND FORMS NEEDED TO FILE FOR BENEFITS FROM ORGANIZATIONS

- Certificate or other evidence of membership
- Policy or other proof of benefit
- Certified copy of death certificate
- Copy of your marriage certificate

(Ask the organization if other information documents are needed.)

CIVIL SERVICE BENEFITS

If the deceased was a civil service employee, he or she probably carried group life insurance and had various health insurance coverages under the Federal Employees Health Benefits Program. The beneficiary of this life insurance receives the proceeds on this policy. Furthermore, a spouse and dependent children may be able to continue their valuable coverage under the health insurance plan, either on a group policy basis or through conversion to an individual policy.

There are also survivor annuities available to the widow/widower and dependent children of a covered employee. The amount of the annuity depends on the spouse's length of service and his or her highest level of income. The widow's annuity will continue for life unless she remarries. A dependent child's annuity will continue until he or she reaches age eighteen (twenty-two if in college).

FILING FOR BENEFITS

For detailed information about eligibility for benefits and how to apply for them, contact any federal agency or send letter 9 to Office of Personnel Management, Civil Service Death Benefits, P.O. Box 45, Boyrs, PA 16017.

DOCUMENTS AND FORMS NEEDED TO FILE FOR CIVIL SERVICE BENEFITS

- A certified copy of the death certificate
- Copy of your marriage certificate
- Copy of both your birth certificates
- Copies of the dependent children's birth certificates

(Ask what other information and documents are needed.)

Other Concerns

DEBTS

In our credit-oriented economy, any person is apt to have a number of debts at the time of death. Probably the deceased was no exception. However, there are several reasons that you should not rush to pay off these debts. Consider the following:

- Your spouse's debts are not your obligation unless the two of you assumed them jointly. His or her debts will eventually be settled when the estate is probated.
- Certain debts may be covered by the deceased's credit life insurance. When the debtor dies and the creditor is notified, the creditor can collect the insurance proceeds to pay off the balance of the loan. Examples are automobile payments, bank credit card payments, installment loans, and department store accounts.
- You may need ready cash for your immediate expenses, as discussed earlier.
- Some obligations attributed to your spouse may be questionable. **Check with your advisor before paying anything.**

WILLS

Many people have not written wills because they think wills are for persons of wealth, older people, persons who wish to give specific items or funds to special organizations or congregations, and those who wish to disinherit someone. This way of thinking is wrong! Anyone who owns anything at all and cares what happens to his or her property at the time of death needs to have a will.

As mentioned in the introduction, this workbook *does not* take the place of a will. The following suggestions may help you in your procuring a will.

- See a lawyer; don't do it by yourself.
- Let someone close to you know where copies of your will can be found (see page 8).
- If you move from one state to another or buy property there, make sure the will meets that state's requirements.
- Review your will and legal arrangements every few years to keep up with changing laws, deaths of beneficiaries, and financial holdings.
- Don't forget worthy causes or organizations (i.e., churches, charities, schools, missions, etc.). Churches often have memorial requests that your gift could provide for while at the same time leaving your name to a specific sacramental or program need.
- If you make a new will, remember that a new will does not automatically supplant the old one. You might like to keep the old copy, but indicate that it has been superseded by the new will.
- Reconsider your choice of executor regularly. Choose someone who is well enough to carry out the duties of an executor. Give the executor complete flexibility. Be candid with your feelings.
- If you want to disinherit someone, be very explicit. Disgruntled family members have often been able to convince the court that the deceased was not of sound mind when the will was drawn up.
- Don't wait to get this done.

If the deceased died intestate, the court will probably appoint an administrator to settle his or her estate. The administrator, likely to be the spouse or a person of the family's choosing, would then be responsible for performing virtually the same duties as an executor.

FINANCIAL CONSIDERATIONS FOR THE FUTURE

- Automobile
- Emergency fund
- Home budgeting
- New credit
- Children's education
- New will

Part III
Letters to Help in Applying for Survivor's Benefits

Part III is designed to help take some of the confusion away from applying for survivor benefits. It is composed of sample letters followed by fill-in-the-blank letters. The fill-in-the-blank letters are intended to be removed from the book and sent to the appropriate agency.

Survivor Benefit Application Letters

LETTER 1—HEALTH INSURANCE COMPANY

Use this letter if the deceased had an individual hospitalization, major medical, excess major medical, or other type of special health insurance policy. The letter should be completed either by the named beneficiary or by the person acting on his or her behalf.

LETTER 2—LIFE INSURANCE COMPANY

Use this letter if the deceased had an individual life insurance policy, annuity, accident insurance policy, or disability income insurance policy. The response to this letter will state what documents and records will be needed to file for the claim.

LETTER 3—CURRENT EMPLOYER

Use this letter to obtain benefits from the deceased's employer. The letter is to be completed by the deceased's spouse, children, and so forth, or by the person acting on their behalf.

LETTER 4—FORMER EMPLOYER

LETTER 5—SOCIAL SECURITY OFFICE

LETTER 6—VETERANS ADMINISTRATION

Mail to closest Veterans Administration center:
Veterans Administration
Regional Office
See United States government listing in telephone book

Forms sent in response to this letter will state what documents and records are needed to file the claim.

LETTER 7—VETERANS ADMINISTRATION (SERVICE-CONNECTED DEATH)

Use this letter if death was service related.

LETTER 8—ORGANIZATIONS

Use this letter to obtain (or inquire about) benefits from any organizations or groups of which the deceased was a member.

LETTER 9—CIVIL SERVICE COMMISSION

Use this letter if the deceased was a civil service employee.

Survivor Benefit Application Letters

LETTER 1

(Date) _____

(Health Insurance Company Agent)

_____

(Address) _____

_____

Gentlemen:

My late *(husband, wife, etc.)* _____ had a *(type of policy)* _____ with your company. *(Name of deceased)* _____ was insured under policy number *(policy number)* _____ and died *(date of death)* _____.

Please send me whatever forms I should fill out in filing a claim for benefits on behalf of either the estate of *(deceased's name)* _____ or *(beneficiary name[s])* _____ survivors.

Sincerely yours,

(Your name) _____

(Your address) _____

_____

_____

Survivor Benefit Application Letters

(Date) _____

_____

_____

_____

Gentlemen:

My late _____ , had a _____ with your company. _____ was insured under policy number _____ and died _____ .

Please send me whatever forms I should fill out in filing a claim for benefits on behalf of either the estate of _____ or _____ _____ survivors.

Sincerely yours,

(Your name) _____

(Your address) _____

_____

_____

LETTER 2

(Date) _____

(Life Insurance Company Agent)

_____

(Address) _____

_____

Gentlemen:

My late *(husband, wife, etc.)* _____ had a *(type of policy)* _____ with your company. *(Name of deceased)* _____ was insured under policy number *(policy number)* _____ and died *(date of death)* _____ .

Please send me whatever forms I should fill out in filing a claim for benefits on behalf of either the estate of *(deceased's name)* _____ or *(beneficiary name[s],* _____ _____ survivors.

Sincerely yours,

(Your name) _____

(Your address) _____

_____

_____

Survivor Benefit Application Letters

(Date) _____

_____

_____

_____

Gentlemen:

My late _____ had a _____

with your company. _____ was insured under policy number _____

_____ and died _____.

Please send me whatever forms I should fill out in filing a claim for benefits on behalf of either the

estate of _____ or

_____ survivors.

Sincerely yours,

(Your name) _____

(Your address) _____

_____

_____

Survivor Benefit Application Letters

LETTER 3

(Date)_____

(Employer)_____

(Address)_____

_____

Gentlemen:

My late *(husband, wife, etc.)* _____, an employee of your company, died on *(date of death)* _____ .

Would you please review your personnel files and other records to determine what benefits might be payable to *(his/her)* _____ estate or beneficiary(ies)? Among other things, such benefits might include group life insurance, hospitalization and major medical insurance, disability income insurance, pension or profit-sharing plan, worker's compensation, deferred compensation arrangement, accrued vacation or sick pay, payroll savings or stock-purchase plan, and credit union balance.

I am writing you on behalf of *(name of deceased)* _____
as beneficiary. If there are any forms to be completed in filing for these benefits or if you need any documents or additional information, please let me know.

Sincerely yours,

(Your name) _____

(Your address) _____

_____

_____

Survivor Benefit Application Letters

(Date) _____

_____

_____

_____

Gentlemen:

My late _____, an employee of your company, died on

_____.

Would you please review your personnel files and other records to determine what benefits might be payable to _____ estate or beneficiary(ies)? Among other things, such benefits might include group life insurance, hospitalization and major medical insurance, disability income insurance, pension or profit-sharing plan, worker's compensation, deferred compensation arrangement, accrued vacation or sick pay, payroll savings or stock-purchase plan, and credit union balance.

I am writing you on behalf of _____
as beneficiary. If there are any forms to be completed in filing for these benefits or if you need any documents or additional information, please let me know.

Sincerely yours,

(Your name) _____

(Your address) _____

_____

_____

Survivor Benefit Application Letters

LETTER 4

(Date) _____

(Former Employer) _____

(Address) _____

_____

Gentlemen:

My late *(husband, wife, etc.)* _____, an employee of your company, died on *(date of death)* _____.

Would you please review your personnel files and other records to determine what benefits might be payable to *(his/her)* _____ estate or beneficiary(ies)? Among other things, such benefits might include a pension or profit-sharing plan.

I am writing you on behalf of *(name of deceased)* _____ as beneficiary. If there are any forms to be completed in filing for these benefits or if you need any documents or additional information, please let me know.

Sincerely yours,

(Your name) _____

(Your address) _____

_____

_____

Survivor Benefit Application Letters

(Date) _____

_____
_____
_____

Gentlemen:

My late _____, an employee of your company, died on

_____.

Would you please review your personnel files and other records to determine what benefits might be payable to _____ estate or beneficiary(ies)? Among other things, such benefits might include a pension or profit-sharing plan.

I am writing you on behalf of _____ as beneficiary. If there are any forms to be completed in filing for these benefits or if you need any documents or additional information, please let me know.

Sincerely yours,

(Your name) _____

(Your address) _____
_____
_____

Survivor Benefit Application Letters

LETTER 5

(Date) _____

Social Security Administration

(Address) _____

_____

Gentlemen:

This is to inform you that my late *(husband, wife, etc.)* _____ died *(date of death)* _____ .

I am writing you on behalf of *(beneficiary* [ies]*)* _____
and would like to obtain an appointment as soon as possible to make application for benefits. Please let me know where and when such a meeting can be arranged.

I will plan to bring the following things with me to that meeting: a copy of the death certificate, a copy of the marriage certificate, copies of birth certificates of the deceased and survivors, the Social Security numbers of the survivors, and evidence of the deceased's recent earnings. If any other information or documents are required, please let me know.

Sincerely yours,

(Your name) _____

(Your address) _____

_____

_____

Survivor Benefit Application Letters

(Date) _____

Social Security Administration

_____

_____

Gentlemen:

This is to inform you that my late _____ died _____ .

I am writing you on behalf of _____
and would like to obtain an appointment as soon as possible to make application for benefits. Please let me know where and when such a meeting can be arranged.

I will plan to bring the following things with me to that meeting: a copy of the death certificate, a copy of the marriage certificate, copies of birth certificates of the deceased and survivors, the Social Security numbers of the survivors, and evidence of the deceased's recent earnings. If any other information or documents are required, please let me know.

Sincerely yours,

(Your name) _____

(Your address) _____

_____

_____

LETTER 6

(Date) _____

Veterans Administration

Insurance Division

(Address from phone book) _____
_____

Gentlemen:

This is to inform you that my late *(husband, wife, etc.)* _____ died *(date of death)* _____ .

(He/she) _____ was insured under policy number *(policy number)* _____

_____ , and I am writing you on behalf of *(name of deceased)* _____ as beneficiary.

(Name of deceased) _____ served in the *(Army, Navy, etc.)* _____ from *(date)* _____ to *(date)* _____ .

Please send me whatever forms should be filled out in making application for the benefits payable under that policy.

Sincerely yours,

(Your name) _____

(Your address) _____
_____
_____

Survivor Benefit Application Letters

(Date) _____

Veterans Administration

Insurance Division

_____

_____

Gentlemen:

This is to inform you that my late _____ died _____ .

_____ was insured under policy number _____, and I am writing you on behalf of _____ as beneficiary.

_____ served in the _____ from _____ to _____ .

Please send me whatever forms should be filled out in making application for the benefits payable under that policy.

Sincerely yours,

(Your name) _____

(Your address) _____

_____

_____

Survivor Benefit Application Letters

LETTER 7

(Date) _____

Veterans Administration

Insurance Division

(Address from phone book) _____

_____

Gentlemen:

This is to inform you that my late *(husband, wife, etc.)* _____ died *(date of death)* _____ .

(Name of deceased) _____ served in the *(Army, Navy, etc.)* _____ . I am writing you on behalf of *(name of deceased)* _____ to apply for any veteran's pension or other benefits that might be due *(him/her)* _____ .

Please send me whatever forms should be filled out in making application for the benefits payable under that policy.

Sincerely yours,

(Your name) _____

(Your address) _____

_____

_____

Survivor Benefit Application Letters

(Date) _____

Veterans Administration

Insurance Division

_____

_____

Gentlemen:

This is to inform you that my late _____ died _____.

_____ served in the _____.

I am writing you on behalf of _____ to apply for any veteran's pension or other benefits that might be due _____.

Please send me whatever forms should be filled out in making application for the benefits payable under that policy.

Sincerely yours,

(Your name) _____

(Your address) _____

_____

_____

Survivor Benefit Application Letters

LETTER 8

(Date) _____

(Organization's name) _____

(Address) _____

_____

Gentlemen:

This is to inform you that my late *(husband, wife, etc.)* _____ died *(date of death)* _____ . *(Name of deceased)* _____ was a member of *(name of organization)* _____ . I understand that *(he/she)* _____ and dependents may have been eligible for certain benefits for *(burial/education/family)* _____ .

I am writing you on behalf of *(name of deceased)* _____ as beneficiary. Please send me whatever forms should be filled out and the necessary instructions for making application for benefits.

Sincerely yours,

(Your name) _____

(Your address) _____

_____

_____

Survivor Benefit Application Letters

(Date) _____

_____

_____

_____

Gentlemen:

This is to inform you that my late _____ died .

_____ was a member of _____ .

I understand that _____ and dependents may have been eligible for certain benefits for

_____ .

I am writing you on behalf of _____

as beneficiary. Please send me whatever forms should be filled out and the necessary instructions for making application for benefits.

Sincerely yours,

(Your name) _____

(Your address) _____

_____

_____

LETTER 9

(Date) _____

**Office of Personnel Management
Civil Service Death Benefits
P.O. Box 45
Boyrs, PA 16017**

Gentlemen:

This is to inform you that my late *(husband, wife, etc.)* _____ died *(date of death)* _____. *(He/she)* _____ worked as a civil service employee from *(date)* _____ to _____.

I am writing to you on behalf of *(name of deceased)* _____ to apply for any pension or other benefits that might be due *(name of survivor[s])* _____.

Please send me whatever forms should be filled out and the necessary instructions for making application for benefits.

Sincerely yours,

(Your name) _____

(Your address) _____

_____

_____

(Date) _____

**Office of Personnel Management
Civil Service Death Benefits
P.O. Box 45
Boyrs, PA 16017**

Gentlemen:

This is to inform you that my late _____ died _____.

_____ worked as a civil service employee from _____

to _____ .

I am writing to you on behalf of _____

to apply for any pension or other benefits that might be due _____.

Please send me whatever forms should be filled out and the necessary instructions for making application for benefits.

Sincerely yours,

(Your name) _____

(Your address) _____

_____

_____

Notes